Western Lullaby

Lynn Estes Friess • Barbara Leonard Gibson

Ⓜ Mariposa Ranch Press

"Come on, honey, it's time for bed," calls Mom.

"Go to sleep my little cowgirl.
It's time to rest your weary head.

The mountains are painted dusky gray
and the moon's come out to play.

In the distance hear the coyote's call,
softly echoing o'er the plain...

telling everyone that night time's
come again with a gentle refrain.

So close your sleepy eyes my
love and cuddle next to me.

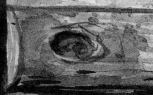

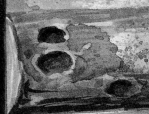

Your momma and your daddy dear
will keep you safe and near.

And as the moon
dances high, across
the diamond sky...

the cowboys croon
this lovely tune,
a *western lullaby.*

Snuggle down beneath the covers, close your eyes and dream sweet dreams...

of the buffalo and the antelope
a runnin' through mountain streams.

And as the lantern light grows dimmer,
a quiet hush is everywhere.

So sleep tight cowgirl,
good night little one...

for now the day is done."

CODE OF THE WEST

FOR LIL' POKES©

Live each day with a smile.

Be the best in all you do.

Finish what you start.

Do what has to be done.

Be honest and fair.

Keep your promises.

Ride for the brand.

Talk less and say more.

Never forget, some things
can't be bought.

Know when to stop.

Mixed Sources
Product group from well-managed
forests, controlled sources and
recycled wood or fiber
www.fsc.org   Cert no.   BV-COC-080720
©1996 Forest Stewardship Council

ILLUSTRATED BY Barbara Leonard Gibson
DESIGNED & PRODUCED BY
Verve Marketing & Design™; Chadds Ford, PA 19317
www.vervemarketinganddesign.com
PUBLISHED BY Mariposa Ranch Press, LLC;
P.O. Box 9790, Jackson, WY 83002
www.mariposaranchpress.com

Library of Congress Cataloging .... pending